AF413474
THIS JOURNAL BELONGS TO

"Live in each season as it passes; breathe the air, drink the drink, taste the fruit, and resign yourself to the influence of the earth."

"Rather than love, than money,
than fame, give me truth."

"If you have built castles in the air, your work need not be lost; that is where they should be. Now put the foundations under them."

"Every morning was a cheerful invitation to make my life of equal simplicity, and I may say innocence, with Nature herself."

"A man is rich in proportion to the number of things which he can afford to let alone."

"I find it wholesome to be alone the greater part of the time. . . . I love to be alone. I never found the companion that was so companionable as solitude."

"A single gentle rain makes the grass many shades greener. So our prospects brighten on the influx of better thoughts."

"All men want, not something to do with, but something to do, or rather something to be."

"If one advances confidently in the direction of his dreams, and endeavors to live the life which he has imagined, he will meet with a success unexpected in common hours."

“However mean your life is, meet and live it; do not shun it and call it hard names.”

"All change is a miracle to contemplate, but it is a miracle which is taking place every instant."

"I had three chairs in my house; one for solitude, two for friendship, three for society."

"A lake is a landscape's most beautiful and expressive feature. It is Earth's eye; looking into which the beholder measures the depth of his own nature."

“The surface of the earth is soft and impressible by the feet of men; and so with the paths which the mind travels.”

ISBN 978-1-4549-6431-5

Union Square Gift books may be purchased in bulk for business, educational, or promotional use. For more information, please contact your local bookseller or the Hachette Book Group's Special Markets department at special.markets@hbgusa.com.

Printed in India

2 4 6 8 10 9 7 5 3 1

unionsquareandco.com

Cover design and illustration by Michelle Merlin
Interior design by Kaylie Pendleton

Endpapers background: Andy Magee/Shutterstock.com